JEFFBECK
GUITARSTYLE

The Complete Authorised Guide to the Soloing Mastery of Guitar Legend Jeff Beck

DANI**RABIN**

FUNDAMENTAL**CHANGES**

Jeff Beck Guitar Style

The Complete Authorised Guide to the Soloing Mastery of Guitar Legend Jeff Beck

ISBN: 978-1-78933-442-5

Published by **www.fundamental-changes.com**

Copyright © 2024 Dani Rabin

Edited by Joseph Alexander

www.fundamental-changes.com

For over 350 free guitar lessons with videos check out:

www.fundamental-changes.com

Join our free Facebook Community of Cool Musicians

www.facebook.com/groups/fundamentalguitar

Tag us for a share on Instagram: **FundamentalChanges**

Cover Image Copyright: Author photo used by permission.

Contents

About the Author 4

Foreword by Jennifer Batten 5

Introduction 6

Jeff Beck Biography 7

Get the Audio 9

Get The Video 9

Chapter One: Twenty Jeff Beck Licks 10

Chapter Two: The Right Hand 23

Chapter Three: Using the Whammy Bar and Volume Knob Melodically 34

Chapter Four: Taps, Slides, and Harmonics 53

Chapter Five: Beck's Pentatonic Scales 60

Chapter Six: Jeff Beck's Rhythmic Approach - Polyrhythms and Phrasing Techniques 67

Chapter Seven: Putting it all Together in a Blues 84

Chapter Eight: Example Solos on a Slow Blues 94

Conclusion 100

About the Author

Dani Rabin is one of the most prolific fusion guitarists recording today. In the last thirteen years he, and his band Marbin, have released 13 albums which include over 150 original compositions. They have played over 2,000 shows worldwide and amassed a cult-like following on social media. Dani is known for his genre-defying playing style, drawing from jazz guitarists like Django Reinhardt and Pat Metheny, as well blues and rock guitarists like Stevie Ray Vaughn and Jeff Beck.

Dani has performed and recorded with artists as diverse as Billy Corgan, Allan Holdsworth, Dennis Chambers, Scott Henderson, Paul Wertico, Jimmy Haslip, Antonio Sanchez, Steve Rodby, Wayne Krantz, and many more.

Foreword by Jennifer Batten

Some of the most elusive elements of music that move us as listeners, and that we all strive for as players, are wrapped up in mystery and surprise.

One of the greatest ongoing goals any improviser can have is to dig deeper and deeper into one's own personality – far beyond scales, arpeggios, influences and styles learned – to unveil and express one's deepest emotions in an original way. Many guitarists, who are lucky enough to find what they feel is their voice, remain somewhat stagnant once they've arrived there. Jeff never stopped digging and inventing.

He once told me about his only two official music lessons, which were with a piano teacher. He hated it. Then he proceeded to explain the difference between acoustic piano and electric guitar, and how the guitar had so much more to offer in the aspect of personalization, with a thousand different conscious and subconscious decisions that go into executing ideas.

Jeff could pull you in with a sonic whisper of extreme sensitivity, then pummel you with the most wicked sounds ever pulled out of a guitar, and everything in between. He was perpetually dissatisfied, and thus continued to push past his own plateaus, always reaching for something new; constantly listening for inspiration from any source, never wanting to repeat what he'd discovered previously.

I locked into his striking musical personality in the 70's and, at one point, I learned every solo on the *Blow by Blow* and *Wired* albums. I used to feel such joy playing along with those records, and I think that was equally as valuable as all of my music training. There is such a wealth of education, just in expression alone, in his records.

I only wish I'd had *this* book back then, as Dani exquisitely takes you by the hand, breaking down some of Jeff's most stunning and incredibly personal elements of the voice he was forever in the process of honing throughout his lifetime. Any one of these elements presented is an invitation to take your expression to a new level. In the end, transmitting emotion is what connects you to your audience and leaves you satisfied. In this course, you will feel what you're learning. Watch and listen to the videos so beautifully executed, get inspired and soak it up!

Jennifer

Introduction

Welcome to an immersive journey into the musical genius of Jeff Beck, one of the most innovative and influential guitarists of all time. This book is designed for guitar players who want to capture the essence of Jeff's unique playing style and incorporate elements of it into their own musical expression. Here you will find detailed analysis, practical examples, and guided practice sessions, and embark on a path to discover the subtleties that made his guitar work so profoundly impactful and timeless.

Anyone who has heard Jeff Beck's music will know he had the ability to effortlessly combine technical prowess with emotional depth – a rare gift. Central to his mastery of the guitar was his unique use of the whammy bar. More than a tool for adding vibrato and pitch bending to his lines, Jeff coaxed vocal-like inflections and nuances that breathed life into each note. His ability to make the guitar *sing* captivated audiences and influenced generations of guitarists. This book will guide you through the steps needed to develop and refine that technique, to add limitless dynamic expression to your playing. We will also explore the broader aspects of Jeff's exceptional tone, dynamic control, and use of space/silence in phrasing to tell a story with his music.

Polyrhythms played a significant role in Jeff's musical vocabulary, adding a sophistication and unpredictability to his compositions and solos. Through practical exercises and examples drawn from his repertoire, you will learn how to integrate polyrhythms into your playing, enhance your rhythmic feel, and create more engaging and complex musical passages.

Jeff's improvisational style was characterized by its fluidity and spontaneity, and this will also be a focal point of the book. You'll learn how to break free from conventional scales and patterns to develop your own voice, following Jeff's strategies for navigating the fretboard with confidence and creativity.

Our hope for this book is that it will be a tribute to Jeff Beck's great legacy. Beyond that, we trust it will provide a clear roadmap for guitarists who desire to reach new heights in their musical journey. Whether you are a seasoned player looking to add nuance to your voice, or an advancing player wanting to break out of a rut, the lessons in these pages will challenge, inspire and guide you to a deeper understanding of mastery of the guitar.

Jeff Beck Biography

Geoffrey Arnold "Jeff" Beck was born in 1944 in a suburb of London, England, and began playing guitar in his teens with a borrowed instrument. Like several other English guitarists of his generation, he attended an art college while becoming actively involved in local bands. Influenced by players like Les Paul and guitarist Cliff Gallup's recordings with Gene Vincent and The Blue Caps, Beck also listened to blues players such as B.B. King. In his early years, he became something of a session guitarist before joining his first notable group, The Yardbirds (where he replaced Eric Clapton on the recommendation of Jimmy Page) in 1965.

Beck played with The Yardbirds for just under two years and recorded one studio album with them in 1966, but was eventually fired during a US tour for missing gigs and having a rather temperamental attitude. Upon leaving this group, Beck recruited Jimmy Page and Keith Moon to record *Beck's Bolero*, which was followed by two solo singles: *Hi Ho Silver Lining* and *Tallyman*. His next group was The Jeff Beck Group which included a young Rod Stewart on vocals. They recorded two albums, *Truth* (1968) and *Beck-Ola* (1969), before disbanding in July 1969. Beck then teamed up with drummer Carmine Appice and bassist Tim Bogart to form a rock power-trio but the project was interrupted after Beck was badly injured in a car crash. He later returned to work with them before the group dissolved in 1974.

By the mid-1970s Beck had produced two instrumental albums (*Blow by Blow* and *Wired*). These showcased his unique approach to the electric guitar in a series of stunning instrumentals, influenced by the jazz-rock movement prevalent at the time. These are still considered among his best recordings. He released three studio albums in the 1980s and was involved with numerous different studio projects and guest appearances.

From the 1990s onward, Beck produced high-quality solo albums at a much higher rate than in past decades. He toured regularly until his untimely death, and is widely regarded as one of rock's greatest and most individual-sounding guitar players.

At various points in his career, Jeff used both Gibson Les Pauls and Fender Telecasters, but it is undoubtedly his long association with the Fender Stratocaster that is cemented in our collective image of him. Fender's Custom Shop produces a Jeff Beck model made to his exact specifications. His Stratocasters were modified to allow considerable up-pull on the tremolo arm, giving him the ability to create sounds only dreamed of by other players. His amplifiers were generally Marshall or Fender and although he used some effects, his hands and the instruments he played were responsible for most of his tones and radical sound changes.

Beck's playing style was utterly unique and he frequently manipulated the tremolo arm to produce tones reminiscent of a slide guitarist or pedal steel player. An excellent example of this technique is the track *Where Were You* from the 1989 album *Jeff Beck's Guitar Shop*. He also frequently used harmonics (both natural and artificial) to great effect within a melody line and favoured volume swells and fast tremolo picking/right-hand tapping.

In contrast to many mainstream rock guitarists, Beck constantly manipulated the guitar's volume and tone controls to change the tone of his instrument while performing. His slide playing and tremolo arm manipulation was astonishingly accurate in terms of intonation, and he used it to recreate non-Western melodies on guitar such as the track *Nadia* from his 2001 album, *You Had It Coming*.

Jeff Beck's sad passing at the age of 78 on January 10th, 2023, was not just a deep blow to guitarists, it was a staggering loss to the entire world's music community.

He was a true visionary and an iconic musician.

Suggested Listening:

Jeff Beck Group – *Truth*

Solo – *Jeff Beck's Guitar Shop*

Solo – *Blow by Blow*

Solo – *Emotion and Commotion*

Get the Audio

The audio files for this book are available to download for free from www.fundamental-changes.com. The link is in the top right-hand corner. Click on the "Guitar" link then simply select this book title from the drop-down menu and follow the instructions to get the audio.

We recommend that you download the files directly to your computer, not to your tablet, and extract them there before that adds them to your media library.

For over 350 free guitar lessons with videos check out:

www.fundamental-changes.com

Join our free Facebook Community of Cool Musicians

www.facebook.com/groups/fundamentalguitar

Tag us for a share on Instagram: **FundamentalChanges**

Get The Video

Due to the nature of Jeff Beck's lose rhythmical style, many of the examples in this book, particularly the whammy bar section, are extremely difficult to notate clearly. For this reason, we have included dozens of video examples to accompany the notation.

We highly recommend that you view these along with the notation as they give depth and insight to the nuances of Jeff's playing that can't be captured by mere lines on a page.

You can access them by visiting

https://geni.us/jeffbeckvideos

Or by scanning the QR code below:

Chapter One: Twenty Jeff Beck Licks

Let's dive straight into the world of Jeff Beck's sound with 20 examples that showcase his unique techniques over static one-chord vamps.

These licks are placed first deliberately, because we felt it was important to start with the music, not the technique. Some of these ideas will be challenging, daunting even, and may represent the end of your journey rather than the beginning, but don't be phased by this. Here we are looking at the kinds of ideas that are possible, having mastered the fundamentals. You can skip this section for now and return later, having worked through the rest of the book.

Watching the included video examples is crucial, as Beck's nuances are often better learned visually and aurally than through notation alone. The link to the video content is on the previous page.

Example 1a begins in the B Minor Pentatonic. Place your index finger on the 7th fret of the G string. As you strike the note, introduce a slight, out-of-tune bend by pulling the string very slightly downwards, before playing the E note on the 9th fret. This motion is played using a "4 over 3" rhythm and the repeated microtonal bends produce a "crying" sound.

Use the whammy bar to scoop into the A on the 10th fret by pushing the bar down just before you strike the note (shown in the video). Follow this with a pull-off to the 7th fret and a whammy bar-assisted bend down a half step. Release the whammy as you scoop into the 7th fret on the G string and resolve to the tonic B on the 9th fret of the D string. Conclude with a dive on the last note – a signature Beck articulation that adds a distinctive "falling" sensation to the end of the phrase.

This four-note sequence, a frequent element in Beck's music, requires diligent practice to master the technique. We'll cover this more in chapters two and three.

Finally, dive with the whammy bar on the final note of the phrase.

Example 1a:

Starting in B Minor Pentatonic and transitioning to B Mixolydian, this line marries the soulful depth of blues with the exotic nuances of Indian music. The shift broadens the tonal landscape and infuses the phrase with an other-worldly character.

One technique critical to capturing Beck's sound is mastering the *ghost-note rake* followed by a whammy bar dip. Here, a sweeping thumb motion across muted strings precedes the tremolo arm manipulation. This subtle yet complex manoeuvre demands precise timing and a light touch but will add depth and texture to your playing.

The technique involves three distinct uses of the tremolo arm, each serving to bend the pitch at carefully measured intervals. The first dip lowers the pitch by a half step, while the subsequent two lower it by a whole step. Practice this idea with a focus on achieving accurate intonation.

Example 1b:

This example starts with a thumb rake leading into a whammy bar dip, timed to land on the downbeat with a half-step dip. This technique demands precision to synchronize the sweep with the tremolo effect.

The line features "2 against 3" rhythms to add a rhythmic contrast that develops the groove. The second measure introduces whammy scoops that are played by dipping the bar as the notes are picked to lend a lyrical quality to the line.

Harmonically, we are moving between B Major and B Minor Pentatonic scales, blending tonalities as is common in the blues.

Example 1c:

In this alternating lick, use your thumb and index finger to switch between the 17th fret on the E string and a bent 18th fret on the B string, allowing both notes to resonate. Ensure your hand is free from the whammy bar during the line.

For the final note's vibrato, press down rapidly with your right hand palm, directly onto the bridge. This is a trademark Beck technique, often applied following rapid thumb and index finger alternation.

The rhythmical interplay of four over three – 1/16th-notes over a 12/8 blues groove – creates a captivating sound.

Example 1d:

This line introduces an Aeolian sound using the b6 of the scale, then adds a bluesy feel by targeting the b5. It's an excellent exercise for integrating whammy bar use with legato techniques like pull-offs and hammer-ons.

Pay attention to the way you scoop into the b5 notes (10th fret on the G string), which are followed by two pull-offs, highlighting the importance of mastering left-hand legato in conjunction with whammy bar effects on single-string passages. The phrase concludes with a dive on the last note.

Example 1e:

This fast-paced line is an excellent exercise for honing your alternating thumb and index finger picking technique. Focus on the repeated pattern in the first bar, using your index finger for picking followed by a thumb pull-off. Gradually practice this segment to ensure an even rhythm.

In the second bar, palm vibrato is applied on the double-stops. This repeatedly sharpens the note and creates a distinctive texture.

This time, the rhythm uses an eight against three pattern to create a compelling effect.

Example 1f:

Starting in B Minor Pentatonic before shifting to B Mixolydian, this line emphasizes a B major triad with an added suspended 4th. Incorporating this tonality within a blues framework creates an Eastern quality often explored by Beck.

The use of the whammy bar is sparing and applied in just three strategic points, demonstrating how minimalistic articulations can profoundly impact expression.

Scoops are played as grace notes leading into their respective pitches without occupying distinct rhythmic space.

A four against three polyrhythm is again used to add rhythmic complexity.

Example 1g:

Beck's approach to tapping diverged from the norm. He set aside the typical continuous fast arpeggios, preferring to play syncopated rhythms using small intervals, which introduced a complex, almost chaotic texture to his phrasing.

In this example, the transition from tapping to cleanly striking a bent note on the 9th fret of the G string poses a significant challenge. Practice this segment slowly, focusing on precision and control.

The line concludes with a rapid, pentatonic legato sequence typical of Beck, showcasing his ability to craft flowing, cascading endings to his lines. This technique, henceforth called *trailing off*, is a signature aspect his expressive language.

Example 1h:

In this example, a straightforward B Minor Pentatonic phrase is augmented with sliding double-stops, which contrast beautifully with the triplet groove in the latter half of the measure. The use of straight 1/8th note rhythms alongside these elements adds a dynamic layer to the line. Adding vibrato and articulation to double stops, especially with a distorted tone, significantly enhances the overall sound.

Example 1i:

This phrase unfolds via a "question, question, question, answer" structure. Each of the first three measures contains similar rhythmic motifs that find resolution in the fourth measure.

In the opening bar, the *Beck Manoeuvre* is used. This is a triad in which we bend down the fifth by a half step on the B string. Then we release the bend while holding the third on the G string as we allow both notes to ring before finishing by playing the root.

Here, a B minor triad is enriched with whammy bar articulations. The line progresses as the second bar ascends the neck to move into a D major triad, followed by a further shift in the third bar to a B major shape.

The resolution comes in the fourth measure, revisiting the initial motif an octave higher and culminates with a sequence of chromatic passing tones set in a 4 over 3 rhythm. The use of complex rhythms allows the integration of dissonant notes to feel organic and harmonically consonant.

Example 1j:

The distinctive feature of this line is the series of half-step whammy bar dips, meticulously timed to inject a vibrant, colourful twist into what would otherwise be a standard descending scale run. Additionally, the line's rhythmic interest is heightened by beginning and ending on an off-beat.

Example 1k:

This line offers a fantastic opportunity to develop fluid phrasing that seamlessly incorporates the whammy bar with pull-offs. It begins with an A major arpeggio, where the major 3rd is bent down to the minor 3rd to capture a bluesy feel. This is followed by a descending A Dorian run, embellished with strategic whammy bar dips for expression.

A notable characteristic of this line is its initial octave, where the higher note is scooped into – another Beck trademark technique.

Example 1l:

This line begins with an A major vibe that swiftly transitions into A minor with question and answer phrasing. A standout feature in the first bar is its mimicry of a harmonica sound – a technique Beck frequently used. The effect is achieved by dipping a note on the B string, then scooping into the subsequent note on the G string as the bar is released, allowing both strings to resonate together. The illusion of slightly detuned strings harmonizing as the bar is lifted offers a bluesy sound that is pleasing to the ear.

The notation includes a "T" on the note at beat one of measure one, signalling a hammer-on-from-nowhere, followed by a pull-off, a manoeuvre often used alongside the whammy arm to craft those harmonica-like tones.

The example also features a cascade of sextuplets in the second bar which will be challenging for those unaccustomed to using their thumb for picking. This passage requires mastering rapid thumb downstrokes paired with pull-offs – a technique that will require some practice, as Beck never used thumb upstrokes.

Example 1m:

Beck loved to use harmonics and this example shows how a compelling line can be crafted using just one string, ascending the harmonic series in a sequence of three-note triplets. To achieve a crisp, resonant quality with each note, use your index finger in an upstroke motion near the bridge. When playing lines rich in harmonics, imagine your index finger as the pick, to ensure each upstroke is snappy and precise.

Example 1n:

This example opens with an arpeggio that mimics a harmonica, this time set within a minor framework. Pay special attention to the 1/16th note triplets at the end of bar one – a rhythmic motif frequently used by Beck that delivers significant impact at this tempo.

The line showcases a comprehensive array of whammy bar techniques, including dips, scoops and vibrato to enrich the melody with dynamic expression. Notably, just before the fourth beat of bar one, there's a scoop into a bent note that adds an exquisite layer of colour.

Example 1o:

In this intricate line, the technique transitions between two right-hand positions within the same lick. Notably, in bar three, following the use of palm vibrato and the subsequent release of the whammy bar, we move to alternating thumb and index finger picking for the remainder of the phrase.

The lick begins with a double-stop, bending the lower note to create tension, then weaves through a series of triads. It transitions from a D major shape at the 14th fret to another D major position around the 10th fret, shifts down to a C major shape near the 8th fret, then circles back to the familiar territory of a root position A Minor Pentatonic box.

An idea like this illustrates Beck's mastery in navigating the fretboard using varied chord shapes, while maintaining a cohesive musical narrative.

Example 1p:

This line begins with thumb downstrokes and hammer-ons, and transitions from 1/16th notes to sextuplets using alternating index finger and thumb strokes. Notice that the note on the B string remains static while the notes on the high E string keep changing. Allow both notes to ring at the same time during the sextuplet figure for added grit.

The concluding double-stop features a whammy bar dive, accentuated by a vigorous, quick brushing motion with the thumb. Achieving a clean execution requires proficient left-hand muting to avoid unwanted string noise, due to the broad motion involved.

Example 1q:

Viewing the video of this line is crucial due to the complexity of the whammy bar technique, which is challenging to capture in notation but clear when seen. Observe the aggressive plucking of the double-stop with the index and ring fingers, accompanied by a wide motion to engage the whammy bar.

To create a *tremolo vibrato*, place the palm of your right hand on the whammy bar and make a karate-chop motion in an 1/8th note triplet rhythm, to produce a distinctive stuttering effect.

Example 1r:

Our next phrase requires behind-the-nut pinches in conjunction with whammy bar dives played rhythmically to give the line a conversational, question-and-answer feel.

Use the middle and ring fingers of the left hand to pinch the G and B strings behind the nut, then dive with the whammy bar to produce a scream between typical blues phrases. Note that this won't work if you have a locking nut!

Example 1s:

This line begins with an A minor arpeggio, highlighted with a singular whammy bar dip, before it transitions into a series of natural harmonics.

One of the coolest neck tricks is dipping the whammy bar down while letting multiple harmonics ring on different strings. The cacophony of notes beating against each other creates a texture that is pretty wild, and magically brings a low pitch into the mix by some miracle of physics.

Example 1t:

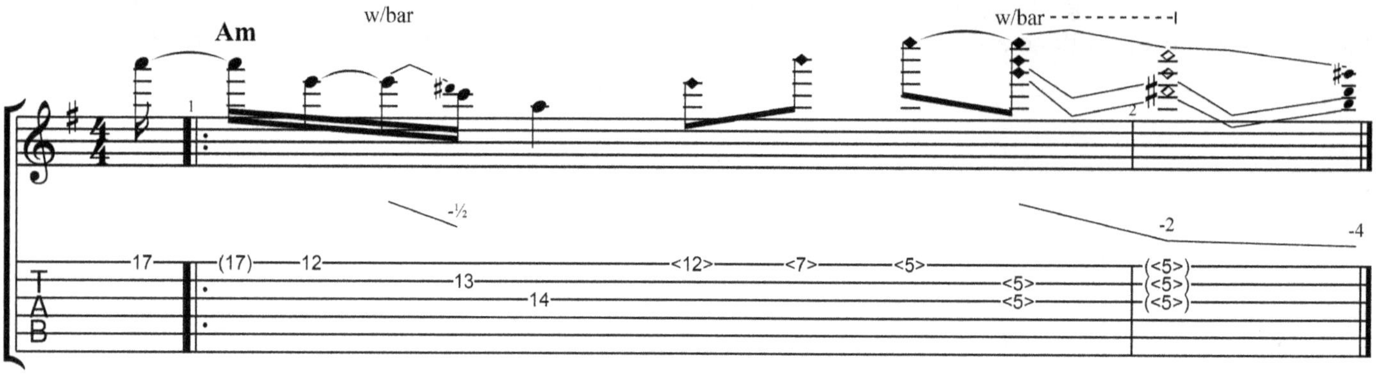

Chapter Two: The Right Hand

Having set the scene with a collection of aspirational licks, from this chapter onwards we'll begin to look more closely at Beck's technique, beginning with the intricacies of his right hand. We'll uncover the secrets behind his dynamic touch and precise picking, along with the expressive control of his palm techniques.

Here we'll explore a series of exercises specially tailored to help you master the nuances that can be achieved through thumb and index finger picking, adjusting right-hand positioning, and adding whammy bar articulation and dynamics via volume knob swells.

The cornerstone of Beck's style lies in the power and texture of the sound produced by the thumb and we'll explore that "fat" note quality that defines his musical voice. Crucial to our studies is Beck's use of dynamics. In general, you should be aiming for a moderate attack of 5 on a scale of 1-10. On a Strat with standard gauge strings, the goal is to extract the richest sound possible without causing the string to snap against the fretboard. This will help you find that sweet spot of dynamic intensity.

In terms of hand placement, one of Beck's primary techniques revolves around a resting the index finger on the whammy bar with the pinkie and ring fingers gently curling around the volume knob. Copying this approach is more than mimicry – it's about finding balance and the connection with your instrument.

In the first example, a G minor arpeggio serves as a practical starting point. Focus on the precise point where the thumb will strike the string, and aim for a location that balances string tension with accessibility to the whammy bar and volume knob. This sweet spot will vary based on your string gauge and action, and requires attentive listening and adjustment to replicate Beck's tone.

To play this line, I use thumb rest strokes when moving from a lower to higher string (allow your thumb to push through the string and rest on the adjacent string until it is time to pluck it), and free strokes going in the other direction. For reference, look at the technique used by the majority of Gypsy jazz players: downward sweeping and upward free strokes.

A G minor triad is the framework for this exercise but you can apply it to any one-note-per-string pattern.

Example 2a:

In the next iteration of the exercise we expand the idea into a two-notes-per-string pentatonic scale. The focus here should be to achieve a fat, round sound. When you achieve that tone, notice the pressure and placement you used in your picking. Keep using rest strokes on the downward string changes and keep working on your consistency and control.

It's vital to get a great sound while keeping your hand in the right place to use the whammy bar. Your picking technique must be solid before you add whammy bar articulation. I often find that if something sounds sloppy in my line, nine times out of ten I need to clean up my picking rather than work on my whammy bar skills.

Example 2b:

```
Gm
T|------------------------------3--6--10--8----------------------|-----------------------|
A|--------------------3--5--3--6------------8--6--7--5------------|-----------------------|
B|--------5--3--5---------------------------------------8--5------8--5----------|
          3--6                                                         8--6
```

Exploring the G Dorian mode across the fretboard is a valuable exercise, not just for scale mastery but for practicing tone refinement. The idea here is to play familiar, automatic movements, so that we are free to focus entirely on the sound we're producing. Alternating between two and three notes per string will be enough to prevent the picking hand from falling into repetitive patterns.

Embrace "evenness" as your mantra during practice. Aim for a pristine first note, then endeavour to match each subsequent note to this standard. This concentrated practice method is not designed for performance, but to refine your touch through subconscious programming.

Example 2c:

```
Gm
T|---------------------------------------3--5--6--3--5--6--8--10--8--6--5--3-------------------|
A|-----------------------2--3--5--3--5--6-------------------------------6--5--3--5--3--2--------|
B|------3--5--3--5-------------------------------------------------------------------3--5------|
        3--5--6
```

This exercise enhances the G minor arpeggio from Example 2a with volume swells on each note. Beck often added swells to individual notes rather than a sequence of notes within an arpeggio. Start by practicing each note's swell to get comfortable with the amount of adjustment needed on the volume knob while plucking.

For a more natural swell, begin with the volume knob set around 2 or 3, rather that starting from silence. Each guitar reacts differently, so use your ears to find the optimal starting point for your instrument. Practice rolling the volume all the way to 10 and aim for a smooth ramp up in volume for each note.

The goal of this technique is to learn Beck's smooth, emotive build, similar to that of a violinist. It's one of his most expressive techniques and mastering it will add a powerful layer of expression to your playing.

Example 2d:

In this variation, we blend the approach from Example 2b with volume swells on alternate notes. Notice that fully opening the volume knob requires some plucking hand repositioning, so that the thumb is placed to hover approximately over the bridge pickup for every other note. This adjustment is crucial to maintain the integrity of the technique and ensure a seamless transitions between notes.

Example 2e:

Next, we'll use the technique from Example 2c on a descending modal pattern and add a volume swell to the first note on each string. I recommend taking any scale you know and practicing it using this technique.

Whenever there are three notes per string, the thumb will shift position to over the bridge on every second note, and move back for the third note. Once you're comfortable with this movement, increase the challenge by adding pull-offs post-swell instead of picking each note. This adaptation allows you to play faster passages that commence with a pronounced swell.

Example 2f:

The next example is reminiscent of the jazz standard *Summertime* played in the rubato style often employed by Beck. Here, we use only volume swells, thumb picking, and traditional vibrato. As you'll hear, this approach alone is powerful, before we even consider adding any whammy bar articulation.

Experiment by varying the intensity of the volume swells on different notes to create dynamic contrast and make your playing more vocal. Swelling to a level of 6 or 7 can yield a sparkling, clean guitar tone to enhance the line's lyrical quality.

This technique will create peaks and valleys in your dynamics and make your phrasing more lyrical. Engaging with these subtle expressive variations will enrich your playing, and gradually these nuances will unconsciously appear in your playing.

Example 2g:

When playing fast double-stop lines, Beck typically released the whammy bar to allow him to alternate picking between his thumb and index finger on adjacent strings. This technique is effective for rapid sequences in thirds, or for maintaining a pedal tone on a lower string with the thumb while the index finger articulates melody notes on a higher string.

An interesting nuance in the following G Minor Pentatonic example is the incorporation of microtonal bends, subtly sharpening the minor third to add expressive colour.

When using this alternate picking method, keep your wrist anchored on the bridge and don't use any rest strokes. Ensure that both the thumb and index finger move in a diagonal upward motion to avoid unintentional contact with adjacent strings.

Example 2h:

The next example showcases a classic Beck manoeuvre found in many of his solos. Here we are moving minor 3rds in G Dorian, before resolving to the major 3rd and 5th of G (B and D). The intervals are played as sustained two-note chords. This creates a cool effect with the overdriven sound that is refreshing to hear after a long string of single notes in a solo.

Key to mastering this lick is the precision of the left-hand slides, each one rhythmically replacing a thumb stroke. Practice this slowly, moving back and forth between any two double-stops until you can play it evenly.

Even though we're not focusing on the whammy bar in this chapter, I couldn't resist diving it at the end, which is very satisfying when paired with double-stops. If you don't like that sound, we can't be friends!

Example 2i:

Next, a pedal tone on the G string anchors the example while melody notes weave through a G Blues scale played on the B and high E strings with the index finger. This unconventional approach creates a distinct tonal contrast between the thumb and index finger, each producing a unique yet consistent sound. This method emphasizes tone over efficiency to create a unified texture from two distinct timbres.

The rhythm introduces a favoured Jeff Beck polyrhythm: triplets played in pairs. This pattern enhances the bluesy backdrop without veering into overly avant-garde territory. The thumb is plucking between the neck and middle pickups to produce a lush, expansive texture.

Example 2j:

Beck frequently incorporates double-stops in his solos and riffs and here a firm tug with the index and middle fingers creates a distinct popping sound, a crucial element of the desired tone (although moderation is important). Use free strokes with the thumb and a semi-circular upward motion to avoid unintentional muting of adjacent strings.

The rhythm is a three-beat phrase within a 4/4 time signature, which creates dynamic movement around the phrase to grab the listener's attention without straying into overly complex territory.

Example 2k:

Next, the focus shifts to three-string raking played with the thumb, which can be viewed as the Jeff Beck version of sweep picking. This example involves using the thumb to glide through inversions of common major and minor triad arpeggios. A key advantage of thumb raking is that it allows you to simultaneously hold the whammy bar with the index finger and add subtle articulations on the top note of each arpeggio.

Make sure the motion of your thumb is rooted in the joint of your finger to execute each three-note arpeggio, rather than using your entire arm to move from string to string. Save the arm movement to shift to the beginning of each three-note structure.

Example 2l:

Next, the thumb rake is used to articulate a one-note-per-string arpeggio which then moves into familiar pentatonic blues box territory.

The rhythmic application of the rake here creates a syncopated feel by dividing the beat into triplets while omitting the initial down-beat. You can simplify this process by focusing on the destination rather than the starting point. Since the thumb lands on the beat with the final note of the rake, focusing on this final note helps makes the rhythm more intuitive.

Example 2m:

This lick is a simple minor arpeggio with a ghosted rake. Use left-hand muting to dampen the first two notes of each rake to create the desired effect. This technique will add depth to your solo's phrasing. Study slide guitarists like Duane Allman or Derek Trucks, particularly their right-hand technique, to understand when and how to apply the ghosted rake. They often rake with their thumb and play the top note with their index finger.

Example 2n:

This line features another ghosted rake. This is the kind of idea you can easily add to your arsenal of moves to add nuance to your performances. Remember that raking with the thumb allows you to keep hold of the whammy bar, so you can add dips and vibrato to your held notes.

Example 2o:

This example serves as an introduction to left-hand muting, a fundamental technique when using overdriven tones. It demonstrates how to strike all six strings while ensuring that only the desired note rings. If you notice excessive noise during this exercise, work on refining your left-hand dampening. Using inactive fingers to suppress unwanted string noise will significantly enhance your clarity.

Example 2p:

Here's the same idea using a two-note-per-string G Minor Pentatonic scale in root position. It's crucial to practice muting with this shape as it's such an important part of Beck's language.

Example 2q:

Next, the left-hand movement mirrors the previous example but now applied to an ascending scale. The muting here is essential for controlling unwanted noise, enabling you to pick more aggressively with broader thumb motions. The ability to strike without confining your thumb to a single string offers a liberating approach and enhances clarity and expressive potential.

Example 2r:

This example delves into a signature Jeff Beck approach: the creative use of harmonics. For optimal results, switch to your bridge pickup and adjust your tone settings to include plenty of gain, to ensure the notes sustain and stand out prominently. This technique, especially effective on a Stratocaster, showcases the dynamic range of harmonics in Beck's style. It's helpful to memorise the first few notes of the overtone series, so that you can predict the resulting note when positioning your finger over any fret on any string.

12th fret = Octave

7th fret = 5th

5th fret = octave

4th fret = 3rd

3rd fret = 5th

Note that positioning your finger over the 5th, then the 4th, then the 3rd fret on any string creates a major arpeggio with the open string acting as the bass note – a technique Beck often used in his melodies and solos. For the best results, pick near the bridge and use the tip of your index finger. I find that the harmonics resonate most when I use the area where the fingernail meets the skin.

Incorporating the whammy bar to articulate harmonics captures the quintessence of Beck's style. Experiment by adding vibrato, dips, volume swells, and dives to mimic his sound.

Example 2s

I have to admit that as someone who isn't a full-time fingerstyle guitarist, I've always found this technique quite awkward, yet it appears in almost every Beck solo. After the first bend, add tremolo picking using the tip of the index finger as if it were a guitar pick. Like me, you may not be fond of how this feels physically, but it is something you will become accustomed to.

In Beck's playing, this technique is never used for playing lines with moving notes. Instead, it's always reserved for a held note (usually a high one), enhanced with fast, alternating tremolo.

Example 2t:

Chapter Three: Using the Whammy Bar and Volume Knob Melodically

Jeff Beck had a unique ability to make the guitar sing. While no single technique can achieve this by itself, mastering the whammy bar for shaping notes, and the volume knob for swelling them will certainly get you close. It's vital to listen to (and watch) the recorded examples throughout this chapter, as many techniques are counterintuitive and challenging to describe in words.

A proper setup with a floating bridge and low spring tension on your guitar is key, so adjust accordingly. If the whammy bar feels too stiff, ease the tension by loosening the screws or removing a spring.

As you begin to explore these techniques, imagine the possibilities of manipulating a note with the whammy bar. Engage in some air guitar, pressing down on an imaginary bar, while "fretting" a note and vocalizing the pitch changes! The point of this is to connect the physical motion with its sonic outcome, and it will supercharge your ability to integrate the technique into your playing.

Let's dive more deeply into Beck's whammy bar techniques. We'll start with a simple ascending minor arpeggio with a scoop added to each note. Each scoop is a grace note without a rhythmic value, so focus only on playing the 1/4 notes in time. Coordinating the correct pressure and timing on the bar is crucial – too little makes the effect too subtle while too much overshoots the desired sound. Find the right balance by imagining a singer gracefully sliding into each note.

Use scooping sparingly in a phrase. While it can beautifully highlight a target note, overdoing it can detract from your playing and sound like a singer struggling to hit the right pitch.

Example 3a:

Let's expand on this idea and apply it to an ascending two-notes-per-string pentatonic scale. Only scoop into the first note on each string. This approach is more realistic approach, as we don't want to scoop every note all the time.

In the video, notice how my wrist lifts slightly before each whammy bar scoop. This motion engages larger muscle groups and helps to prevent fatigue.

Example 3b:

This example showcases a more nuanced variation of this technique. The focus is on playing the top note of each string group first, then playing a pull-off followed by a scoop to articulate the second note. This combination of pull-off and scoop becomes crucial for capturing the Beck style, offering an alternative to traditional picking methods once mastered.

It's important to recognize that no two scoops will ever sound identical. Each interaction with the bar is an opportunity to uniquely shape the note, allowing personal expression and artistic nuance to enter your playing.

Example 3c:

Let's apply the techniques we've discussed to the first four bars of *Goodbye Porkpie Hat* by Charles Mingus. This melody is particularly suited for practice because it benefits from a rubato approach (played slowly and without strict time) and gives us ample space to navigate the technical nuances of volume swells.

Notice that we use volume swells sparingly here. Selectively choosing which notes to swell allows us to highlight them to enhance the melody and mimic the dynamic control of a skilled vocalist.

Take your time and embrace a relaxed, unhurried pace. Your goal is to breathe life into the notes, transforming a technical exercise into a musical expression that feels as natural and nuanced as singing.

Example 3d:

In the next passage we navigate a descending A Dorian line while adding downward whammy bar bends. While they may resemble scooping in some ways, you will find them more distinct because the bent notes carry specific rhythmic values, as opposed to the grace notes of the scoops.

Intonation is crucial here, and it's significantly easier to play accurate 1/2 step bends than whole tone bends with the bar. For this reason, you should become proficient with 1/2 step bends before exploring larger intervals.

Focus on the technique for the opening three notes: strike the first note (C on the 8th fret of the high E string) with your thumb, then use the bar to bend down a 1/2 step before concluding with a pull-off to the 5th fret. Typically, when combining three-notes-per-string phrases with a whammy bend, I tend to only pick the string once with my thumb.

Example 3e:

The next exercise is perfect for refining your 1/2 step bends musically. Here, we navigate through the A Minor Blues scale, adding 1/2 step bar bends between the 5th and b5th, and from the b5th to the 4th. These intervals represent the blues scale's only 1/2 steps (1, b3, 4, b5, 5, b7).

Ensure you play these bends as straight 1/8th notes and avoid transforming them into grace note dives. To do this effectively, scoop down to the target note then firmly hold the bar in position to sustain the pitch without vibrato. Use your whole arm to press and secure the bar as relying solely on wrist motion will quickly lead to fatigue.

Example 3f:

Let's now explore Beck's use of upward whammy bar bending, a technique that's simpler than downward bending but requires a specific guitar setup. On my Stratocaster, I use two springs in the back and adjust the claw by unscrewing both screws equally until it remains straight. This adjustment allows for the open G string to reach a Bb note (minor third) above when I pull the arm up and the bridge touches the body.

This setup also means that pulling the bar all the way up raises the high E string by a 1/2 step, the B string by a whole step, and the G string by a minor third, making upward bending predictable and giving the guitar a pedal steel-like function.

The line played here uses the A Dorian mode on the high E string, and incorporates upward 1/2 step bends to transition from the 7th fret B to the C at the 8th fret, and from the 14th fret F# to G at the 15th.

It's important to note that after bending, I use a left-hand slide to ascend to the next note. Attempting to pick the note directly after a bend would require releasing pressure on the bridge and an unintended scoop.

Understanding the scalar intervals of the key, and how the bar behaves with upward bends will greatly improve your ability to incorporate this technique into your playing.

Example 3g:

While this example uses the same notes as the previous one, it shifts the A Dorian mode to the B string and this time adds whole-step bends with the whammy bar. This approach is particularly effective, as we alternate between picked notes and bar bends. Specifically, bend from the 10th fret to the 12th (A to B), 13th to 15th (C to D), 17th to 19th (E to F#), and from the 20th to the 22nd (G to A).

Using the guitar setup described earlier, pulling the bar all the way up will always yield a whole step bend on the B string – a useful principle to remember!

Think of pulling on the whammy bar like accelerating a motorcycle by twisting the throttle. The motion mostly involves the wrist and requires considerable practice to perfect.

Example 3h:

In this exercise, we will focus on bending pitches down by a 1/2 step with the whammy bar before bringing them back to their original pitch.

Practice the first eight notes in a loop. The pattern begins with a four-note sequence that is then mirrored on both the high E and B strings. Start by counting a measure in 4/4 time, subdivided into 1/8th notes. On the high E string, play the 8th fret on beat one and bend the pitch down a 1/2 step with the whammy bar on the "and" of beat one. Return to the original pitch by easing off the bar on beat two, then play a pull-off to the 5th fret on the "and" of beat two. Finally, replicate this exact sequence on the B string.

The key takeaway from these exercises is to become rhythmically proficient with the whammy bar, integrating it seamlessly into your playing to create dynamic, expressive, rhythmically interesting lines.

Example 3i:

In this exercise, I add upward 1/2 step bends with the whammy bar that resolve back down to target the two points in A Dorian where half steps occur (B to C and F# to G). The points we are bending from in this mode happen to be the 9th and 13th intervals, which are extremely colourful.

Being able to visualise the intervals in a mode is critical when using the whammy bar as it's vital to bend to a pitch that's in the scale.

Example 3j:

The next idea uses the A Minor Pentatonic scale and showcases a signature Jeff Beck technique. The first measure merges pentatonic boxes two and one and features a whammy bar grace note scoop on the first beat, followed by a rhythmically timed whammy bar bend on the third beat.

The second measure continues with similar bar usage in shape three of A Minor Pentatonic and highlights a D major triad around the 10th fret. The line progresses through shape four in the third measure and concludes in box five by the fourth. Use the thumb for picking and the whammy bar for articulation to emphasise this signature Beck approach.

Example 3k:

The next example showcases a favoured whammy bar technique: a rhythmic reverse bend followed by a hammer-on. The method involves pressing the bar down to lower the pitch by a half step before striking the note. Aim for the detuned note to fill the space of one 1/8th note, with the pitch returning to normal on the next 1/8th note. Following the reverse bend, a hammer-on played that extends over a 1/4 note duration. This two-beat lick is a hallmark found in numerous Beck performances.

Here, I use the notes of the A Minor Pentatonic scale on the B string. Overall, the idea not only highlights Beck's ability to manipulate pitch, but adds a layer of expressiveness and interest that transforms the simple melodies into captivating musical phrases.

Example 3l:

This line, inspired by Jimmy Herring (who originally stole it from Jeff), captures the essence of a guitar mimicking the sound of a blues harmonica. The key feature here is the trill on the B string. Interestingly, we only need to pick the B string at the very start of the line; the subsequent notes are maintained through strategic use of whammy bar scoops in tandem with pull-offs, effectively replacing the need for additional picking. The goal is to master the left-hand trill while judiciously incorporating whammy bar scoops to prevent the notes from losing their sustain.

A useful mnemonic for the rhythm involved in this technique is the word "LineBaCker". It represents the rhythmic pattern of an 1/8th note tied to two 1/16th notes. Envision playing a whammy bar scoop on the "Line" syllable, followed by a hammer-on on "Bc" and a pull-off on "Cker". This verbalisation will help you play the line more precisely.

In the concluding part of the phrase we see the "Beck manoeuvre" again. It begins with a half-step bend down on the B string. While holding this bend, fret and pluck the G string, keeping the B string's note sustained. Both pitches are then simultaneously brought back to their original pitch before striking the note on the D string. This sequence produces a texture similar to a blues harmonica, particularly as the overtones clash in a raw, gritty way as the notes return to pitch.

Example 3m:

The Beck manoeuvre, when isolated and moved through all three inversions of an open A chord across the D, G, and B strings, becomes an important technique when capturing Jeff's style. This approach to handling a one-note-per-string triad was a staple in his repertoire, and its mastery is crucial for anyone aiming to capture his musical language. Dedicate a lot of practice to this technique to ensure a fluid execution.

Example 3n:

To further explore this concept, the following line is a five-note variation on the Beck manoeuvre. Though written in 5/8 time, its typical use is within a 4/4 measure where its repetition introduces a polyrhythmic feel. In this variation, the first note of the three-note sequence is picked, followed by a pull-off, then a whammy bar half-step bend. The sequence concludes with the Beck manoeuvre applied over an A major triad.

Experiment with adding this repeated five note figure to your typical blues box playing in any context or tempo. It will enhance your playing immediately with minimal effort.

Example 3o:

Shifting the right-hand position and dropping the whammy bar to free up the index finger and thumb for picking introduces new possibilities into your playing.

Here, the thumb performs the first three notes, while the index finger articulates the fourth. An important technique here is the palm-on-the-bridge vibrato – a signature articulation Beck used in this hand position. It involves a sideways hand rotation and using the side of the palm (more commonly used for palm muting) to exert rapid pressure on the bridge to create vibrato. This method, albeit demonstrated in an exaggerated form here, is a technique Beck frequently used for both subtle and pronounced effects on both single notes and chords.

As with any vibrato technique, maintaining rhythmic consistency is crucial. Ensure your vibrato motions are both rhythmically stable and uniform in their intensity. Vibrato that dwindles or abruptly returns to a sustained note detracts from the line's musicality.

Example 3p:

The next example builds on the palm-on-the-bridge vibrato idea by adding double-stops played with the index and ring fingers. This technique generates a gritty, swampy sound by simultaneously bending two notes. Given the whammy bar's construction, these notes do not shift in pitch uniformly and results in some intriguing harmonic clashes that, especially with a bit of overdrive, produce a compelling musical effect.

Example 3q:

In this example, an upward whammy bar movement enhances the first note in measures one and three with a broader, more rapid vibrato, more like the traditional finger vibrato used by blues players. This method involves holding the bar with the index finger and thumb, and requires precise timing to add the vibrato after picking the note with the thumb.

Adding a ghosted rake allows a seamless transition onto the whammy bar for the vibrato. Additionally, the lick incorporates cascading two-notes-per-string runs that are played with a thumb pick and followed by a pull-off. You might find these challenging if you don't have a background in fingerstyle.

Example 3r:

In the next example, the approach is essentially the same but with a downward whammy bar vibrato. This is performed by placing rapid pressure on the bar to lower the pitch, creating a sound that uniquely blends the qualities of both tremolo and vibrato. It's a sound effect that truly showcases the versatility of the whammy bar as it produces a sonic texture that can't be replicated by any other means.

To create this vibrato, I rely on two different hand motions depending on the musical context. The first involves using the side of my pinkie finger to press down on the bar, leveraging the weight of my entire arm in a motion like a karate chop for a wider vibrato effect. This technique is useful for achieving a more pronounced dip in pitch.

The second method uses the fleshy part of my middle finger between the joint and the first knuckle to exert pressure on the bar. This approach is particularly effective when creating subtler vibrato effects with a moderate dip as it engages a smaller muscle group and allows more precise control over the vibrato's intensity and rate.

Example 3s:

This idea explores whammy bar dives which were often used by Beck at the conclusion of phrases. This involves playing a note then using the whammy bar to dramatically lower the pitch until it virtually disappears. Typically, a dive serves as a grace note without its own distinct rhythmic value.

Playing dives requires a specific hand positioning. The fingertip of the index finger, along with the middle and ring fingers around their second knuckles, applies the necessary pressure on the whammy bar. We need to exert a considerable amount of force to achieve the full range of the dive, yet be careful not to descend too rapidly. The goal is to allow the pitch to decrease smoothly and evenly, rather than abruptly to achieve the desired effect.

Practicing lines like this is an effective way to master this technique. Crafting exercises that incorporate ascending and descending through a pentatonic scale with a dive at the end of each run will help develop your control and musicality.

Example 3t:

In my opinion, the next three examples are some of the coolest Beck techniques I've heard. They just have a wild sound, and I still remember hearing them as a kid and thinking, "What the hell was that?!"

First, we play natural harmonics at the 5th fret across the D, G, and B strings with a thumb stroke, followed by a pull up on the whammy bar. The essence of this sound is created by the interplay and discord of the harmonics as they shift out of tune at different rates due to the varying tensions on each string.

This method doesn't necessarily align with traditional harmonic structures but rather serves as a sonic effect. Jeff Beck's use of this technique isn't about music theory, it's more about rock 'n' roll; it creates a moment of surprise.

Example 3u:

This example is similar, but focuses on the natural harmonics located at the 4th and then the 3rd frets of the D, G, and B strings. Use the thumb for the initial strike and manipulate the whammy bar to create a dynamic shift in pitch.

This variation continues to explore the interaction between harmonics as they are stretched out of their original tuning to build a rich, layered texture.

Example 3v:

This example repeats the same concept but adds some bar vibrato and a dive on the way out.

Example 3w:

Next, the technique demonstrated in Example 3u is integrated into a typical Beck-style A Minor Pentatonic blues sequence. The unique twist comes at the conclusion of the phrase, where I select a natural harmonic above the 5th fret on the D, G, and B strings, then use the whammy bar to elevate the pitch.

This approach is a dramatic and unconventional method to finish a phrase. Embodying Beck's style means welcoming the unconventional, merging unusual sounds and adding advanced approaches into your repertoire.

Example 3x:

This idea is a Beck-style A Minor Blues lick culminating in a unique resolution that features an upward harmonics whammy bend. Place your index finger over the 4th fret, strike the D, G, and B strings with your thumb, then pull up on the whammy bar to add an expressive flourish to the end of the phrase.

Example 3y:

Exploring Beck's more complex techniques, this example highlights his use of the whammy bar to craft melodies by bending notes in both directions. Here, we focus on melodic *enclosures* in A Dorian on the B string.

An enclosure is a pattern of notes that surrounds a target pitch with notes above and below it. Enclosure notes are often a *scale tone above* and a *chromatic step below*. The pattern used here is:

Original note – *scale tone above* – original note – *chromatic step below* – original note.

Measures one, three and six contain a whole-step bend on the B string. This means that if your bridge is set up in the way described earlier, you can pull the bar up all the way and accurately raise the pitch by a whole tone.

However, the bend in measure five (12th fret on the B string) is a half-step bend up, demanding fine-tuned muscle memory for precise intonation. To master this, visualize the pitch rising as you would sing it. This will help internalise the exact location to halt the bend.

Downward half-step bends to an approach note require a keen ear and developed muscle memory for accurate tuning. You'll need to practice diligently, preferably against a drone note, to gauge your intonation. This method not only enhances your technique but ingrains the essential Beck characteristic of melody-driven whammy bar use.

Example 3z:

In the next line, you'll use all the techniques discussed previously to combine the intricacies of Beck's style. In measure one, the high E note at the 12th fret is initially bent up a half step then released by pulling the whammy bar all the way up to where the bridge meets the body. Measure two features a five-note enclosure similar to those outlined in Example 3y to demonstrate the application of melodic embellishment around target notes.

We continue with additional whammy bar half-step bends in measures three and four. The first bend descends from the 5th to the b5th on the B string, while the second ascends from the 4th to the b5th on the G string. The idea concludes with a minor third bend from the b3rd to the b5th on the G string, which is performed by pulling the bar all the way to the body.

Example 3z1:

In the next example, a *whammy rattle* or *gargle*, is added to each note of a pentatonic scale to create a unique texture. Begin by plucking the note with your thumb. Immediately after, pinch the whammy bar then release it swiftly in a single, fluid motion.

The effectiveness and extent of the rattle can vary significantly depending on the guitar's bridge setup. A setup with less tension, such as a one-spring configuration, tends to produce more pronounced rattle effects. For players drawn to this distinctive sound, adjusting the bridge to reduce tension can amplify the technique's impact, offering a more dramatic expression. This strategy allows for greater customization of the guitar's sound, tailoring its output to the specific aesthetic preferences of the player.

This technique should be used sparingly, as while it can add an interesting dimension to your sound, it can definitely be overused.

Example 3z2:

In the next example, the whammy rattle is used to emphasise the notes in an A Minor Pentatonic scale. The approach is particularly effective when repeating a melody within a song, serving as a dynamic way to restate thematic material. The rattle adds a pronounced, screaming character to the notes, imbuing them with a sense of intensity and purpose.

Example 3z3:

In the final three examples we are going to use the melody of *Twinkle Twinkle Little Star* as a canvas to incorporate the techniques explored in this chapter. Although very simple, it's important to have a solid grasp of the melody before adding articulations, so that we enhance rather than detract from it.

Beck's distinctive articulations and techniques – such as whammy bar manipulations, harmonics, volume swells, and dynamic vibrato – were all built upon a strong foundation of accurate note execution, solid rhythmic feel, and overall sound quality. These latter elements are our "cake" while the articulations are the "icing".

Begin by playing the melody in its purest form and focus on clean execution, rhythmic accuracy, and tonal clarity.

Example 3z4:

Now play the melody again and add volume swells with your right hand wherever you see fit. Don't allow the swells to throw off your rhythm.

On your initial run through the melody, add swells to just a few select notes to introduce dynamics without overwhelming it.

On a second run through, add swells every two beats. This will test your ability to keep the rhythmic structure of the melody while controlling the dynamic changes.

This exercise will not only improve your control over volume dynamics but deepen your understanding of how to use them creatively.

Example 3z5:

Now let's add the whammy bar and bring the melody to life, Beck-style. Here we add scoops and use occasional slides, hammer-ons and pull-offs to get into the scooped notes.

Key Techniques to Incorporate:

Whammy bar scoops: Use the whammy bar to slightly dip the notes before they reach their intended pitch. The scoop should be subtle – enough to add expression without significantly altering the melody.

Slides, hammer-ons and pull-offs: These techniques should be used judiciously to move between notes and add a layer of smoothness and fluidity to the melody.

Example 3z6:

Approach to Practicing These Techniques

Start slow: Begin by practicing the melody slowly, focusing on integrating the whammy bar scoops with precision. Pay attention to timing to ensure that the addition of scoops doesn't throw off the rhythm.

Add complexity gradually: Once comfortable with basic scoops, add slides, hammer-ons and pull-offs. Practice the transitions into these techniques from the scoops maintaining good rhythm.

Focus on timing: The main challenge is keeping the melody in time while adding expressive techniques. Use a metronome to practice, starting slow and gradually increasing the tempo as you become more comfortable.

Aim for intuitive play: The goal is to reach a level of proficiency where these techniques become second nature, allowing you to use them on any melody spontaneously.

By methodically adding these techniques you can transform any simple melody into a dynamic, expressive musical statement.

Chapter Four: Taps, Slides, and Harmonics

In this chapter, we'll explore some of the extended techniques Jeff Beck used as special effects to embellish his lines, as he seamlessly integrated them into his melodies.

Among these techniques, tapping stands out, but Beck had a completely different take on it compared to the flamboyance common in '80s rock, for example. Instead, he often used it to execute rapid, articulated trills to add excitement and texture to his lines.

In this example, a B Minor Pentatonic blues phrase is accentuated with a Beck-style rapid tapping trill between the E and D on the G string. Using Beck's second right-hand position (discussed earlier) allows the use of the index and ring fingers for picking while the palm adds vibrato from the bridge. This style of tapping calls for a smooth movement of the right hand to the tapping point immediately after plucking a note.

Beck's approach highlights the melodic potential of tapping, rather than a fast, technical device. Explore its expressive possibilities in your playing.

Example 4a:

Next, the focus is on slap harmonics.

For those new to slap harmonics, the technique involves holding a chord shape with the left hand while the right hand index finger slaps the guitar strings to create harmonics precisely 12 frets above the fretted notes. This technique is particularly effective with chord shapes that involve barring, as the harmonics can be generated across a straight line. However, with a bit of imagination and practice, even more complex shapes can produce surprising harmonic sounds. The key is to visualise the chord shape 12 frets up and aim for those harmonics with confidence. This example explores slap harmonics over a descending E Mixolydian mode paired with an E9 chord shape.

Example 4b:

While maintaining the single note trilled by the tapping hand, this variation introduces additional dynamics through the left hand with a series of pull-offs. This technique not only breaks up the rhythmic monotony of the melody but also adds a layer of complexity and interest.

Example 4c:

The next example involves playing a chromatic ascending line around a B minor chord framework, using the tapping hand to play a series of half-step trills ascending the neck.

The challenge here is maintaining rhythmic accuracy. To achieve this, notice that each tap on a new note is played on the downbeat while the trills are played as sextuplets.

Example 4d:

This technique is known as a *behind the nut pinch*, a unique guitar trick that gained popularity through performances by artists like Stevie Ray Vaughan, most notably in his rendition of *Riviera Paradise*.

When Jeff Beck uses this technique, it's typically characterised by a grittier tone and often paired with an emphatic dive bomb for dramatic effect. It's an ear-catching sound, but one where excessive use can overwhelm and detract from the music, so use with discretion.

Example 4e:

Using the whammy bar to articulate the melody of *Somewhere Over the Rainbow* presents a formidable challenge and epitomises the intricacies of Beck's style.

A key moment comes in the third measure and requires a level of precision and control that exceeds the typical use of the whammy bar. Bar three begins with a natural harmonic on 12th fret (G). The second beat requires a push on the bar to lower the pitch to an E (a minor third below). This is followed swiftly by another descent to F, all without reverting to the original picked pitch during the line. This sequence demands not just technical skill, but an almost intuitive interaction with your guitar.

The final three notes of this section intensify the challenge, as we must maintain the string's sustain while navigating back to the initial G, bending up a whole step to A, then immediately pressing the bar down to reach an F note – a major third descent from the A.

Example 4f:

Playing *Somewhere Over the Rainbow* an octave higher adds to the challenge and explores the limits of what is achievable with harmonics and the whammy bar. Beck's approach to these melodies was not one of improvisation but of meticulous arrangement, shining a light on his unparalleled mastery of the guitar. This method helps transcend the limitations of the fretboard and helps you access normally inaccessible pitches with natural harmonics.

For example, to reach a high A#, a pitch not readily available on the fretboard as a natural harmonic, Beck would ingeniously combine a 5th fret harmonic on the B string (B) with a precise whammy bar depression to bend the pitch down a half step to A#.

Here, the goal is to end the melodic phrases on a pitch altered by the whammy bar, challenging the player to maintain both accurate intonation and musicality.

Through diligent practice and repetition, these complex techniques will gradually become more accessible, allowing you to accurately perform them in a live setting.

Example 4g:

Jeff Beck occasionally used a slide on his middle finger which was a bit unusual but certainly a comfortable choice. This example gently explores his slide technique.

Throughout, right-hand muting is key. Aim to create a sort of "tunnel" around the B string in which your thumb mutes the E, A, D and G strings and the middle finger mutes the high E. Your index is then free to pick the B string without any unwanted string noise that would be created by the slide touching multiple strings.

Allow your left-hand thumb to come off the back of the neck for long slides, but root it when the pitches are within reach. Here, in order to play in tune, the fingers open up to move the slide from fret to fret.

Example 4h:

Jeff Beck's mastery of *slide tapping* is genuinely astounding for its precision and intonation. To demonstrate this technique, I've chosen to interpret the melody of *Black Orpheus* in E Minor as an apt showcase of its potential.

This approach bears a similarity to slap harmonics, as we must replicate the melody's structure twelve frets higher than its original location on the fretboard. The challenge lies in the absence of physical fret markers in this higher register.

To generate the slide tapping, the slide should be manoeuvred like a computer mouse, gently tapping against the strings at the equivalent of 12 frets higher than the fretted note. Incorporating a swift, lateral vibrato not only enhances the articulation but also cleverly disguises any minor pitch inaccuracies to ensure a smoother performance.

For this technique to work effectively, selecting the bridge pickup is crucial, particularly in capturing the delicate notes of the melody. Without it, the desired clarity and projection is very much compromised.

Example 4i:

Next, let's explore a trick that Steve Vai loves to use which, it seems clear to me at least, he "borrowed" from Jeff Beck! It's all about giving the last few notes a really fat, dramatic scoop that sounds a bit like the note is stumbling home after a drunken night out!

The idea is to hit the note with your thumb and push down on the whammy bar at the same time to bend the note down before it even starts. Then, let it return to pitch for that woozy effect. It might feel weird and take a while to get the hang of this technique at first but stick with it. Once you get it down, it'll add a new layer of cool to your playing.

Example 4j:

Now let's return to *Twinkle Twinkle Little Star* and turn it into a harmonics-only performance. This is a great way to become familiar with the way harmonics are laid out across the fretboard. In this key, the melody can be played exclusively with harmonics, but move a half step in either direction and you'll almost certainly need to come up with an entirely different arrangement. (If you want to play it in another key, you'll need to use the whammy bar to bend some of the harmonics).

This approach is a powerhouse technique to boost your familiarity with harmonics across the entire neck. Watch the video and have fun!

Example 4k:

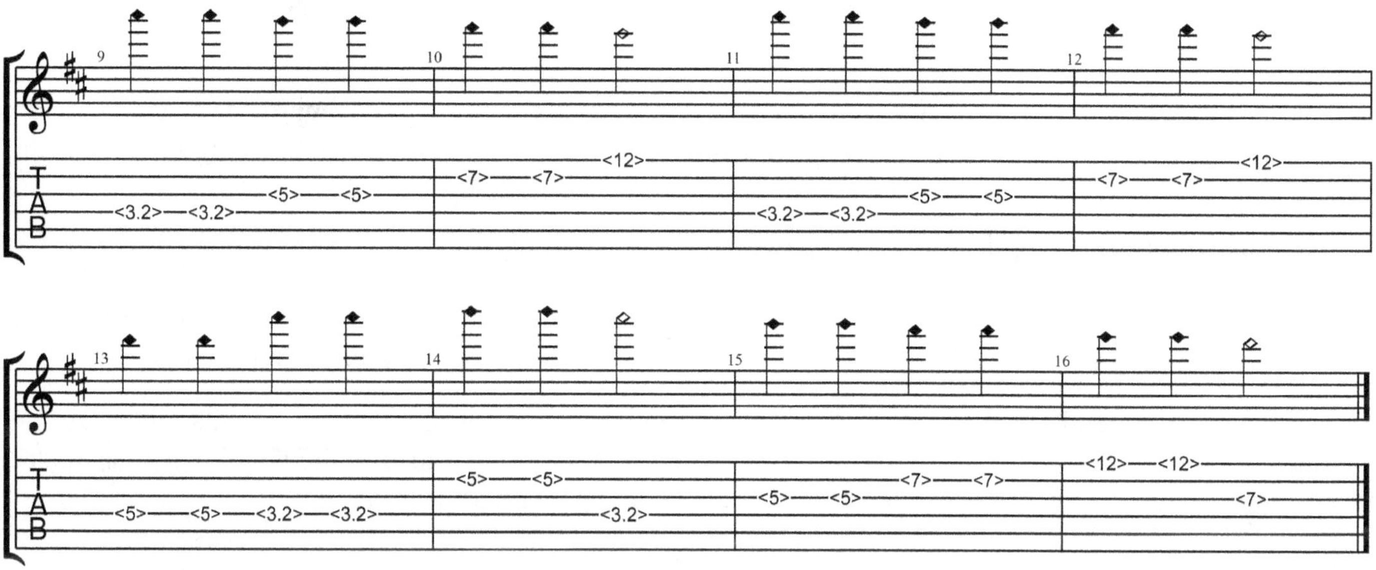
9
10
11
12
T
A
B
<3.2> <3.2> <5> <5>
<7> <7> <12>
<3.2> <3.2> <5> <5>
<7> <7> <12>
13
14
15
16
T
A
B
<5> <5> <3.2> <3.2>
<5> <5> <3.2>
<5> <5> <7> <7>
<12> <12> <7>

Chapter Five: Beck's Pentatonic Scales

Jeff Beck often used exotic sounding pentatonic scales to create melodies and improvise lines. He had a simplified system of being able to extract pentatonics from modal sounds and we're going to look at this idea here.

Consider the Dorian mode, which consists of seven notes: 1, 2, b3, 4, 5, 6, b7.

If we compare this to the intervals of the minor pentatonic scale (1, b3, 4, 5, b7), we can see that, in one sense, the pentatonic scale can extracted or "derived" from the Dorian mode by omitting its 2nd and 6th degrees.

If we apply this principle to each mode of the major scale, we discover that the minor pentatonic scale can be derived directly from three of the modes. Then, if we apply the same idea to the remaining four modes, omitting their 2nd and 6th degrees yields some unique, exotic pentatonic scales.

Ionian (1, 2, 3, 4, 5, 6, 7) becomes the Ionian Pentatonic (1, 3, 4, 5, 7).

Dorian (1, 2, b3, 4, 5, 6, b7) yields the Minor Pentatonic (1, b3, 4, 5, b7).

Phrygian (1, b2, b3, 4, 5, b6, b7) also gives us the Minor Pentatonic (1, b3, 4, 5, b7).

Lydian (1, 2, 3, #4, 5, 6, 7) becomes Lydian Pentatonic (1, 3, #4, 5, 7).

Mixolydian (1, 2, 3, 4, 5, 6, b7) becomes Mixolydian Pentatonic (1, 3, 4, 5, b7).

Aeolian (1, 2, b3, 4, 5, b6, b7) also leads to the Minor Pentatonic (1, b3, 4, 5, b7).

Locrian (1, b2, b3, 4, b5, b6, b7) becomes Locrian Pentatonic (1, b3, 4, b5, b7).

These new pentatonic scales are streamlined versions of their modal counterparts, each with its own characteristic sound.

Let's explore this idea starting with the G Minor Pentatonic scale played over a G drone note. We'll simplify the learning process by focusing on one string to avoid the fretboard's complexity. As you practice, say the intervals out loud as you play them to lay a foundation that will make it easier to transition towards Beck's exotic scales.

Example 5a:

Example 5b uses the Ionian Pentatonic scale, which can be thought of as a minor pentatonic with raised 3rd and 7th intervals. This modification gives the scale an Indian raga flavour, a characteristic often explored by Beck when soloing over major 7 chords.

Example 5b:

The Lydian Pentatonic scale is similar to the Ionian but with a #4 instead of the natural 4. This adjustment lends the scale a mysterious quality with an exotic flavour which Beck frequently used over major 7 chords.

Example 5c:

The Mixolydian Pentatonic scale (differing from the minor pentatonic by just one note, a raised 3rd degree) creates a sound that is effective over dominant chords, making it an excellent option for blues. This scale, with its slight Eastern touch, is often heard in Beck's more exotic blues lines.

Example 5d:

The Locrian Pentatonic scale (differing from the minor pentatonic by its flattened fifth degree) is heard extensively in Japanese music and creates a dark and mysterious vibe. It's particularly fitting for minor 7b5 chords but adaptable to any minor chord, thanks to the b5 acting as the familiar "blue" note. You can also view this scale as a blues scale minus the perfect fifth (1, b3, 4, b5, b7).

Example 5e:

R   b3   4   b5   b7   R   b7   b5   4   b3   R

TAB: 0—3—5—6——10—12—10—6——5—3—0

To learn these scales in the classic root position blues box at the 3rd fret, let's begin with a one-octave G Minor Pentatonic scale starting on the D string. Say the scale intervals aloud as you play them to set this foundational minor pentatonic scale as a reference for the exotic pentatonic shapes that follow.

Example 5f:

R   b3   4   5   b7   5   4   b3   R

TAB: 5 — 3 — 5 — 3 — 6 — 3 — 5 — 3 — 5

For the Ionian pentatonic variation, play a major 3rd (B instead of Bb) on the G string and a major 7th (F# instead of F) on the B string. Practice ascending and descending through this scale against a G drone track to internalise its distinct sound.

Example 5g:

R   3   4   5   7   5   4   3   R

TAB: 5 — 4 — 5 — 3 — 7 — 3 — 5 — 4 — 5

To create the Lydian Pentatonic scale, adjust the minor pentatonic by playing a major 3rd (B instead of Bb) and a raised 4th (C# instead of C) on the G string, along with a major 7th (F# instead of F) on the B string.

Example 5h:

For the Mixolydian Pentatonic scale, modify the minor pentatonic by playing a major 3rd (B instead of Bb) on the G string. This adjustment introduces a versatile sound that's effective over dominant chords with its blend of blues and exoticism.

Example 5i:

For the Locrian Pentatonic, make a subtle yet impactful change to the minor pentatonic by lowering the 5th to a b5 (Db instead of D) on the B string. This adjustment creates a distinctive sound with a dark, mysterious vibe, well-suited for minor 7b5 chords, as well as adding a unique twist to any minor chord sequence.

Example 5j:

Now let's explore some vocabulary around those scales, inside the root position box.

Let's begin with a line based around the G Minor Pentatonic scale using previously discussed foundational techniques (whammy bar scoops and bends, etc).

Example 5k:

In the following example we echo the previous rhythm and articulation but now with a twist: altering the 3rd and 7th intervals to form an Ionian Pentatonic scale, whereby the mood and vibe of the melody shifts dramatically.

Learning this scale will arm you with the appropriate vocabulary to play over major 7 and major 6 chords with a more deliberate sound.

Example 5l:

Let's dive into the Lydian Pentatonic scale, beginning with a straightforward four-note descending sequence. It's beneficial to explore various shapes and patterns within any new scale to acquaint your hands and ears with its possibilities. Similar to the previous example, this scale lends itself well to major 7 chords, adding an exotic flair with its angular #4 interval.

Example 5m:

The Mixolydian Pentatonic was a favourite tool in Beck's arsenal, especially over dominant chords. This example showcases the "Beck Manoeuvre" detailed in earlier chapters, along with some fundamental bar techniques. Once you're comfortable locating this scale on the fretboard, it becomes quite straightforward to mix and match its notes.

Example 5n:

This G Locrian Pentatonic example features a catchy repeating motif embellished with scoops, perfectly fitting for the minor 7b5 chords commonly found in jazz. It can also add a unique twist to minor blues chords. View it as a blues scale minus its natural fifth and it creates an intriguing intervallic texture.

A practical approach to mastering this scale is to visualise the familiar minor pentatonic framework and simply adjust the 5th down a half-step as needed. Fans of Megadeth might recognise this scale's distinctive sound, as Marty Friedman frequently used it to achieve his signature Japanese-influenced solos in many classic metal tracks.

Example 5o:

Chapter Six: Jeff Beck's Rhythmic Approach - Polyrhythms and Phrasing Techniques

This chapter deals with the invisible component that makes Jeff Beck's music so appealing: his use of polyrhythmic lines. His way of improvising phrases that rhythmically relate to one another is simply amazing, and there is much to learn from him on this front.

Each example here is designed to be played over the Funky G Minor Rock backing track in the audio download, which will help you to master the practical application of these techniques.

When tackling Beck-style polyrhythmic lines, the first step is to internalise the rhythm's pulse and subdivisions. In this first example, begin by tapping your foot to the beat, then mentally conceptualise the pace of the 1/32nd notes that slice each beat into eight equal divisions.

In this exercise, we are playing 1/32nd notes in unevenly grouped clusters of three. The idea of pairing uneven groupings with the underlying beat creates a polyrhythm – a rhythmic pattern that cycles and shifts across measures in a captivating dance of melody and timing.

Notice that each triplet pattern is played ten times before the melody moves to a different arpeggio. Harmonically, this example uses a strategy known as *triad pairs,* where two triads from the same scale are combined and alternated between to create the melody. Here, we juxtapose Bb major and C major triads over the G minor groove to create a vibrant tension and release.

Use the index finger to pick the first note and pull-off to the second note before striking the third note on the adjacent string with the thumb. This picking pattern is common in Beck's repertoire of rapid-fire passages.

Example 6a:

In the next example we hit the ground running with rapid 1/32nd notes, this time organised into groups of six. This segment highlights the Dorian mode, with the highest notes alternating between the scale's b7 and 6th degrees to create a rich, modal blues texture.

The right-hand picking mirrors the previous example, and we will use the Indian *solfege* counting system of Solkattu to verbalise each rhythm and internalise its nuances. To help grasp this example, vocalise the syllables "Ta-Ki-Ta" in time with the backing track and match the pace of the 1/32nd notes. If this proves challenging, substitute a fun three-syllable word such as "Ca-Ri-Bou" to make the exercise more accessible.

Polyrhythms can often quickly lead us into uncharted rhythmic territory and tempt us to pause or disengage from the example. The key is to persist and maintain the flow until reaching a rhythmic landmark like a drum beat on the 2nd or 4th beat, which serves as a familiar checkpoint. The sensation might feel like you're caught in a spin, but it's crucial to navigate through it and exit gracefully at the right moment.

Example 6b:

This next idea might seem like a high-speed tapping showcase at first look, but it's this particular type of speed that makes it stand out as we delve into the realm of double quintuplets. This sophisticated rhythmic pattern splits each beat into ten evenly spaced parts to create a dense, intricate texture. The right index finger is responsible for tapping out five of these notes, while the other five come from pull-offs – all anchored by a note held by the fretting hand.

To hear the rhythm, vocalise and say "Ta-Di-Ki-Na-Tum" with each tap of the index finger. The rapid succession of notes makes it impractical to assign a syllable to the pull-offs due to their speed. However, sticking to our playful animal theme, you could articulate this grouping with the word "Hip-po-Po-Ta-Mus", ensuring each syllable coincides with a tap and your foot taps the ground on every "Hip." Begin by syncing this word rhythmically with your foot taps, then add the index finger taps, and finally weave in the pull-offs between the tapped notes. Above all, listen to the audio example and try to play along!

Although this example doesn't quite fall into the polyrhythmic category (as the melody doesn't displace throughout the measure) it leverages a rarely used subdivision to build a compelling rhythmic tension against the groove.

Example 6c:

In this rhythmically packed example, we weave a descending E Diminished triad against the G minor groove. The rhythm structure here is a clever arrangement of 3+3+2. Given that these numbers add up to eight, and we're subdividing in 1/32nd notes, we're not in polyrhythmic territory, just exploring an idea that has great internal syncopation.

To get this rhythm under your fingers and into your ears, vocalise it as "Ta-Ki-Ta Ta-Ki-Ta Ta-Ka" or, continuing with our animal-themed mnemonics, "Ca-Ri-Bou Ca-Ri-Bou Bu-Nny". The critical challenge is to maintain rhythmic precision and ensure each note and syllable is perfectly even and firmly locked in with the groove. The essence of this approach is lost if there's any deviation from set rhythm.

The idea uses the same two triads as the earlier examples, but the final pair brings a new twist. This closing segment can be interpreted as two 1/8th notes concluded with a pull-off, or simply as a sustained 1/4 note on the high Bb. This nuanced variation adds an extra level of interest to the line, and challenges you to keep the rhythmic integrity while navigating the fretboard.

Example 6d:

In this example we stick to familiar G Minor Pentatonic territory on the D and G strings. While the note selection is straightforward, the rhythmic element introduces a fresh challenge. We're still working with rapid 1/32nd notes, but this time grouped into a seven-note pattern divided into segments of 3+4 notes.

To internalise this rhythm, you can vocalise it as "Ta-Ki-Ta Ta-Ka-Di-Mi" or, "Ca-Ri-Bou, Rhi-no-ce-ros". These phrases really help to bridge the gap between understanding the rhythm intellectually and feeling it intuitively.

The three-note group of notes is played with an index finger pick, a pull-off, then a thumb pick. For the four-note group, the pattern expands slightly to become an index finger pick, a pull-off, a thumb pick, and another pull-off. This pattern packs a punch when incorporated into a solo and highlights the exhilarating potential of combining simple pentatonic ideas with complex rhythmic structures.

Example 6e:

Next, we fill a bar with straight 1/32nd notes arranged into two repeating sixteen-note sequences. These are organised into a pattern of 3+3+3+3+4.

To familiarise yourself with this rhythm, practice vocalising "Ta-Ki-Ta Ta-Ki-Ta Ta-Ki-Ta Ta-Ki-Ta Ta-Ka-Di-Mi" or "E-Le-Phant E-Le-Phant E-Le-Phant E-Le-Phant A-lli-ga-tor." These phrases offer a rhythmic blueprint that will help you to internalise the flow of the pattern. It's about embedding the rhythm so deeply that it enhances your overall timing, precision, and rhythmic creativity, enabling you to hear rhythmic options that were previously outside your comfort zone.

Example 6f:

This exercise takes a step back to approach polyrhythms at a more manageable tempo. Here, the focus is on 1/16th notes grouped into threes. In this pattern, you will incorporate the whammy bar, bending it down on every second note of the pattern.

The melody is drawn from G Dorian and features ascending double-stops on the B and G strings – an idea often used by Beck to add texture. This approach adds interest to what would otherwise be a straightforward 1/16th note sequence.

To internalise the rhythm, vocalise "Ta-Ki-Ta Ta-Ki-Ta Ta-Ki-Ta Ta-Ki-Ta" in 1/16th notes along with the groove.

Example 6g:

This is one of my favourite polyrhythms.

This line is another G Dorian idea using ascending double-stops. Here, slow 1/16th notes are organised into patterns of five, which are further subdivided into groups of 3+2. The polyrhythmic texture is enhanced by using the whammy bar to bend the second note in each group of three, mirroring the technique introduced in the previous example.

To familiarise yourself with this rhythm, conceptualise it as a continuous stream of five-count groups *without* the internal 3+2 subdivision i.e., reciting "Ta-Di-Ki-Na-Tum Ta-Di-Ki-Na-Tum Ta-Di-Ki-Na-Tum Ta-Di-Ki-Na-Tum" in sync with the audio track.

Once you're comfortable with this foundational rhythm, dissect it into its 3+2 structure by vocalising, "Ta-Ki-Ta Ta-Ka Ta-Ki-Ta Ta-Ka Ta-Ki-Ta Ta-Ka Ta-Ki-Ta Ta-Ka".

This method of breaking down the rhythm might initially seem complex, but mastering the underlying beat is as crucial as the precision of the notes being played.

Example 6h:

In this passage, we explore a seven-note grouping played at a 1/16th note pace. The novelty here involves the strategic use of the whammy bar on the second 1/16th note within each seven-note sequence.

The seven-note grouping is broken into a pattern of 3+2+2. To grasp this rhythm, repeat, "Ta-Ki-Ta Ta-Ka Ta-Ka" in sync with the backing track. Alternatively, you could view this grouping as a 3+4 pattern, vocalising it as, "Ta-Ki-Ta Ta-Ka-Di-Mi".

This example is anchored in the G Dorian root position, which should be pretty straightforward to visualise. The aim here is to develop a dual focus on both the melodic and rhythmic aspects of playing, enabling you to produce engaging, rhythmically-rich musical lines.

Example 6i:

Now, let's shift into sextuplets (dividing the 1/4 note into six equal slices).

This example helps you master a pattern of two-note groups played with double-stops on the G and B strings. It's a technique that pops up in many Beck solos, and will give your right hand a solid workout because there are no legato notes or whammy bar effects to fall back on.

The key here is smooth picking alternating between the thumb and index finger. Watch out for leaning too heavily on the thumb, as it might mess with your timing and prevent the phrase from fitting snugly into the groove. Use a gentle touch with the thumb and a stronger push with the index finger to create a balanced tone.

Once you're comfortable with the sextuplet feel, loop the rhythm by saying, "Ta-KA Ta-Ka Ta-Ka". Dive deep into this one, it's a treasure trove of musical ideas waiting to be explored.

Example 6j:

In the next idea, the rhythm stays with sextuplets grouped in twos, similar to the previous example. However, this time, every other note comes to life with the whammy bar bending the pitch down a half step and snapping it back in time.

What adds an extra layer of cool to this line is the shift from sextuplets on beats 1 and 2 to 1/16th notes on beats 3 and 4. This transition between subdivisions adds complexity and mirrors the kind of rhythmic variety that made Jeff's playing stand out.

Example 6k:

This line shares a close resemblance with the concept from Example 6j. The twist comes with the introduction of a new note on the B string during the fourth sextuplet of beat 3 in the first and second measures. Although this might appear to be a small adjustment, it significantly alters the line's predictability.

Jeff understood that even with polyrhythmic pattens that weave intriguingly through the measure, listeners will eventually anticipate the flow. Thus, he masterfully added subtle variations to disrupt this predictability and ensure the melody kept its freshness and appeal.

Example 6l:

```
w/bar
        3                                    4
TAB:
  -1
  7------5------8----5----3------3----10----5------3
                       5
```

This example showcases a fascinating polyrhythm with a group of ten notes played in a sextuplet rhythm. The melodic pattern is a descending five-note sequence in G Dorian played by the index finger while the thumb consistently pedals a G note in between. This interplay between the complex polyrhythm and the melodic pattern creates a kind of "spinning" effect.

Example 6m:

```
Gm                                                              w/bar
1                                     2                     3
    6      6      6      6               6      6      6      6
                                                                   -3
TAB:
13-12-10------13-12-10------13-12----10------13-12-10------13-12-10----11
      13-11------13-11------        13-11------13-11------13
12-12-12-12-12-12-12-12-12-12-12--12-12-12-12-12-12-12-12-12-12-12
```

Now we'll explore some question-and-answer phrasing. In the previous examples we looked at interesting ways to create motion in a busy melody line by using a variety of speeds and subdivisions, but now we'll take a closer look at the relationship between phrases, and how to make melodies sound related by using space to create melodic symmetry.

This example contains a two-bar phrase that ends with a sustained note on the downbeat of bar two, then a second phrase that is almost identical rhythmically. There are three things you should notice about this:

- The rhythm in measures one and three is identical

- The empty space in measures two and four is almost identical

- The first phrase resolves to the b3rd and the second phrase resolves to the root

These elements create a call and response structure, which always helps listeners to engage more with the music, and the use of silence is as important as the notes we play.

Example 6n:

$\quad$ = 120

Gm

(music notation - tablature, Gm, w/bar markings)

You can also craft a *sequence* of melodic musical questions, as demonstrated below. This sequence consists of repeating one-bar phrases with a brief pause on the fourth beat. The concept here revolves around posing three questions followed by an answer in the fourth measure. It's crucial that the final notes of each question do *not* hit the root note, so that the phrasing can be resolved by the "answer".

Example 6o:

Gm

(music notation - tablature, Gm, w/bar markings)

Now, let's explore an eight-measure phrase divided into four two-bar phrases, applying the same principle as the previous example. Here, we extend the concept by crafting two-measure phrases instead of single-measure ones, and weave together three musical questions by using similar rhythms in measures one, three, and five, while introducing symmetric pauses in measures two, four, and six.

When we revisit the melodic motif from measure one in measure three, using triplets instead of 1/16th notes, the phrases continue to mirror each other, creating a *rhyming* effect. The power of this idea lies in the echoing motifs and coherent musical ideas rather than the mechanical repetition of rhythms. Let's train our minds to grasp this concept, as it becomes quite straightforward to play once fully understood.

Example 6p:

Now look at this eight-bar phrase that splits into two four-bar sections, each comprising three questions and one answer. Take note of the rhythmic construction of the phrases. Measures one, two, three, five, and six all feature the same rhythmic figure and identical space on the final two 1/16th notes of the bar.

There are numerous ways to approach phrasing, but it's wise to start with one, two, and four-measure motifs as the foundational elements. You can gradually introduce more complex choices as you progress.

Example 6q:

In the next few examples, we'll delve into Beck's approach to rubato playing, a technique I often refer to as "floating the rhythm". While I've attempted to capture what was played in notation, merely reading it won't fully convey the essence of the technique, so do check out the audio. The core concept revolves around loosening your rhythms against the backdrop of the groove, in the same way that legendary vocalists such as Frank Sinatra or Billie Holiday floated over the musical pulse when performing a ballad.

This approach allows for a rhythmic freedom that enhances lyrical expression, offering a level of expressiveness that is deeply impactful when done properly. To really grasp this technique, listen to the recorded examples and watch the accompanying videos for the next three examples.

Example 6r:

This line is a little more aligned with the rhythm grid than the previous one, but the rhythms are still played with considerable flexibility. The aim here is to create a sense of gradual acceleration and deceleration against the groove, especially when moving between different subdivisions.

This style of playing is particularly effective at slower tempos and at the start of a solo, where it can add a dynamic, expressive quality.

Example 6s:

Here you'll need to lean heavily on your listening skills because the rhythm is loosely interpreted. Don't focus on subdividing the beats too strictly, but keep a feel for the overall pulse. In other words, keep things rhythmic but in a smoother, more flowing manner. Think of it as the difference between a break dancer and a ballet dancer moving to the same song. Here, we're aiming for the ballet dancer's approach: interpreting the rhythm with graceful, rounded movements that flow towards the beats.

Example 6t:

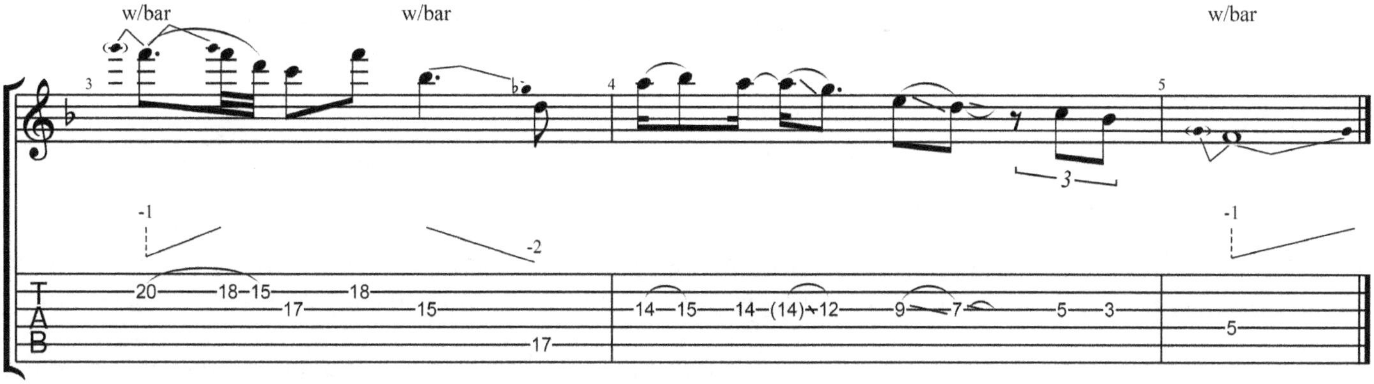
w/bar
w/bar
w/bar
-1
-2
-1
T
A
B

Chapter Seven: Putting it all Together in a Blues

In this chapter we're going to bring together all the techniques we've studied so far and apply them to a I IV V blues progression in C. If you encounter any technical challenges, pause and revisit the earlier sections where these techniques are broken down in detail.

The first example uses the Beck manoeuvre (which was extensively explored in Chapter Three), across each chord of the blues progression, and involves playing a descending arpeggio starting on the b7 of each chord.

Phrasing-wise, the first eight measures are structured around two-bar question and answer motifs, while the final four measures consist of a sequence of one-bar phrases. Working through this example will equip you with a practical structure for outlining chord changes and help you to step beyond the common blues-rock strategy of relying on a single pentatonic scale for the entire progression.

Example 7a:

Next, we delve into creating question and answer phrasing in a more traditional blues context by structuring our lines into four-bar melodies. We start with a four-bar phrase and follow it with another similar phrase that responds to the first, then conclude with a variation that brings a sense of conclusion.

This example is built around a double-stop played as a two-note grouping in a triplet rhythm to craft a distinctive polyrhythm in measures one, two, five, six, ten, and eleven. This technique, especially when enhanced with heavy vibrato, echoes the classic slide blues sounds of legends like Muddy Waters and Howlin' Wolf.

Keep the whammy bar in easy reach for the vibrato, scoops, and dives. The transitions between the regular playing position and reaching for the bar may present some challenges initially, but with consistent practice they should become more comfortable and fluid.

Example 7b:

This is one of my absolute favourite Jeff Beck whammy bar licks. At its core, it's a simple three-note pattern that cycles and begins with a whammy bar scoop. This is followed by a hammer-on then a pull-off.

To get this right it's important to start slow. Only pick the first note in the bar, letting the whammy bar scoop create the string vibration for the subsequent notes. We're essentially using the bar as a substitute for the pick.

Rhythm-wise, this idea is structured around a nine-over-two polyrhythm. It starts with 1/4 note triplets (think of these as 1/2 notes divided into triplets) then breaks these down further into threes, which creates eighteen evenly spaced notes across each measure.

This lick uses a similar phrasing approach to previous examples, with three four-bar phrases that create a call-and-response effect by echoing rhythms and balancing space to build a musical conversation.

Example 7c:

In this example, the phrasing adopts a consistent rhythmic motif in the first two bars of each four-bar segment (specifically in measures one, two, five, six, nine, and ten). Note the contrast in rhythmic patterns between measures three and four versus measures seven and eight, and likewise between eleven and twelve.

This method of structuring phrases over a blues form offers a balance of symmetry and variation, which allows a more dynamic and less monotonous improvisation in the intervening two bars. This style of phrasing, reminiscent of classic big band arrangements, often features a few horns laying down the "question" in the first half of each phrase, followed by a "response" from the soloist to form the dialogue in the music.

Example 7d:

This 12-bar example uses a nice blend of the techniques we've covered. In the first eight measures, the melody is broken into two four-measure phrases that establish a question-and-answer dynamic, enhanced by some expressive whammy bar articulations. In the final four bars the rhythm transitions into a rubato feel. This shift introduces a lyrical quality to the melody and is a great contrast to the 1/8th notes and triplets that dominated the earlier measures.

Listen/watch the example and notice the point at which the melody is freed from the constraints of the groove. This treatment of time is an essential component of all good blues playing as well as central to Beck's style.

Example 7e:

By dividing the first eight measures into two distinct four-measure phrases, this next example subtly weaves rhythms that, while sharing common elements, do not mirror each other exactly. This method exemplifies a more advanced stage of phrasing, where the essence of a line is captured and echoed to achieve a call-and-response effect, rather than relying on exact repetition.

The final four measures introduce chromatic passing tones that add a jazz-like quality to the melody. These tones, particularly effective over the G7 chord in measure nine, draw from the G Mixolydian mode. The inclusion of chromatic passing tones (adding a note between the whole steps of the scale) serves to add tension and release to the melodic line.

Example 7f:

In the next example, the focus shifts to applying a polyrhythmic structure explored in Chapter Six. Here, a distinctive double-stop riff unfolds over the first four measures, using a seven-note grouping within a triplet framework. This approach results in a rhythmic pattern that crosses bar lines, creating a compelling tension. This tension builds until the pattern finds resolution on the downbeat of the fifth measure.

Notice the strategic use of rubato towards the line's conclusion. This slight deviation from strict timing may seem subtle, yet it significantly impacts the overall feel and injects a moment of freedom and expressiveness after the strict polyrhythms. Momentarily stepping outside the rhythmic structure acts as a musical "exhale" and provides a refreshing contrast to the rhythmic complexity.

Example 7g:

Here, the focus is again on using question and answer phrasing effectively over the first eight bars of a 12-bar blues, breaking them into two four-bar phrases to create a conversational structure.

In the final four bars, a distinct rhythmic tension is introduced with the straight 1/16th notes, which push against the shuffle groove. Since the shuffle is based on a triplet feel, using subdivisions that are not divisible by three (like 1/16th notes), creates a powerful tension. This technique is especially noticeable in the pentatonic 1/16th note runs against the shuffle and shows how playing against the groove can add rhythmic interest to our performance.

Example 7h:

The next rhythm involves alternating between the notes of a double-stop in sextuplets. This sounds great because the higher note, played with the index finger, naturally stands out at fast speeds.

This pattern is used in the first two measures of each four-bar phrase to set up a question and answer structure. Then, starting at measure nine, the index finger is used like a guitar pick to produce a tremolo effect.

Example 7i:

The beginning of this final question and answer sequence features some classic Beck motifs and the Beck manoeuvre within the first four bars. By measure five, an Ebmaj7 arpeggio over the F7 chord introduces a jazzy chord substitution that adds sophistication to the blues improvisation. Halfway through measure six, there's a shift in right hand positioning that enables better access to the bridge for some palm vibrato effects. An additional nuance to observe in this passage is the whammy bar upward vibrato in measures nine and ten.

Example 7j:

Chapter Eight: Example Solos on a Slow Blues

We conclude our journey with three improvised solos for you to study over a slow, 12/8 blues in G, using all the techniques and concepts discussed throughout the book. While the inspiration from Jeff Beck's style is evident, these solos are original interpretations and aim to show how you can incorporate these ideas into your own playing style, rather than simply emulating Jeff's licks.

Given the slow tempo of a 12/8 blues, there's ample space within each measure to explore a rhythmically diverse approach that might be challenging to understand through notation alone. I recommend you listen closely to, and watch, the recorded examples multiple times before attempting these ideas.

Example 8a:

G7
w/bar
tapping trill
D7
full
C7
w/bar
w/bar
G7
w/bar
w/bar
full
D7
w/bar
w/bar

Example 8b:

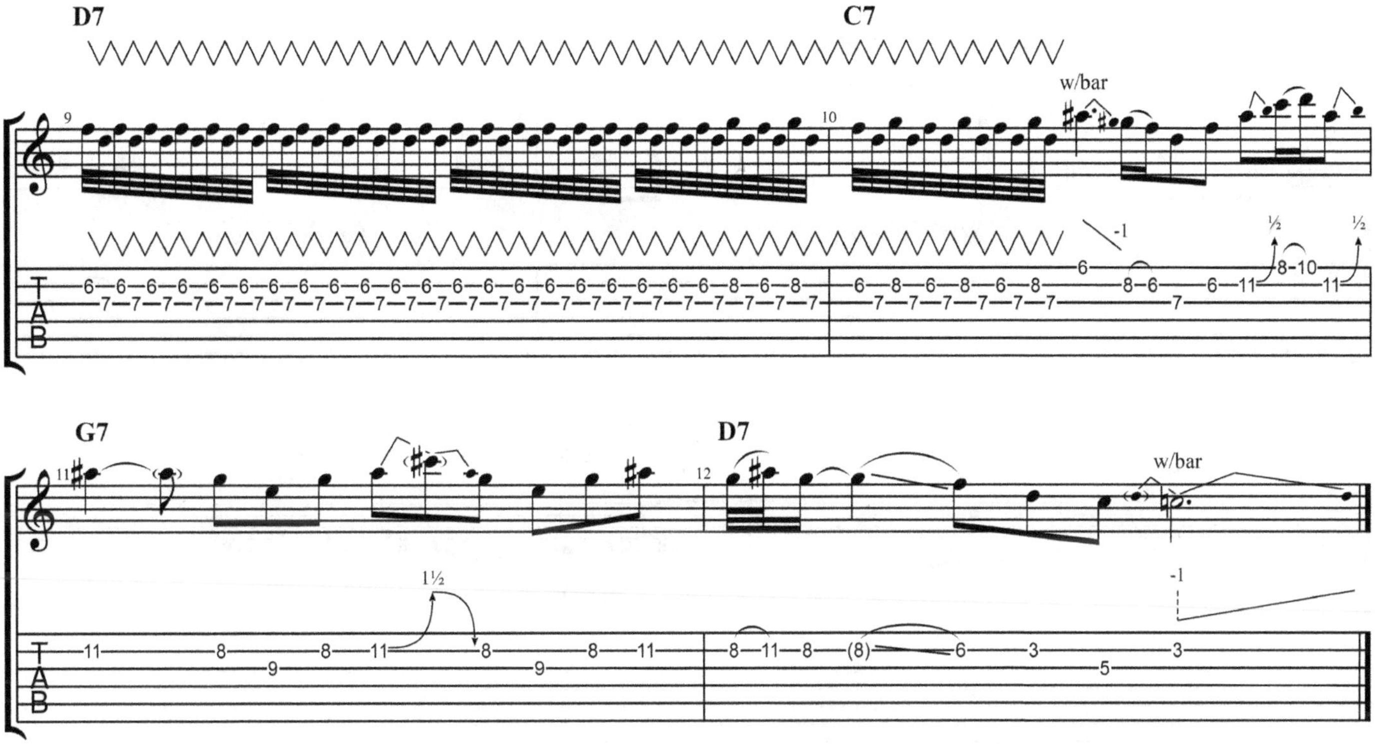
D7
C7
w/bar
G7
D7
w/bar

Example 8c:

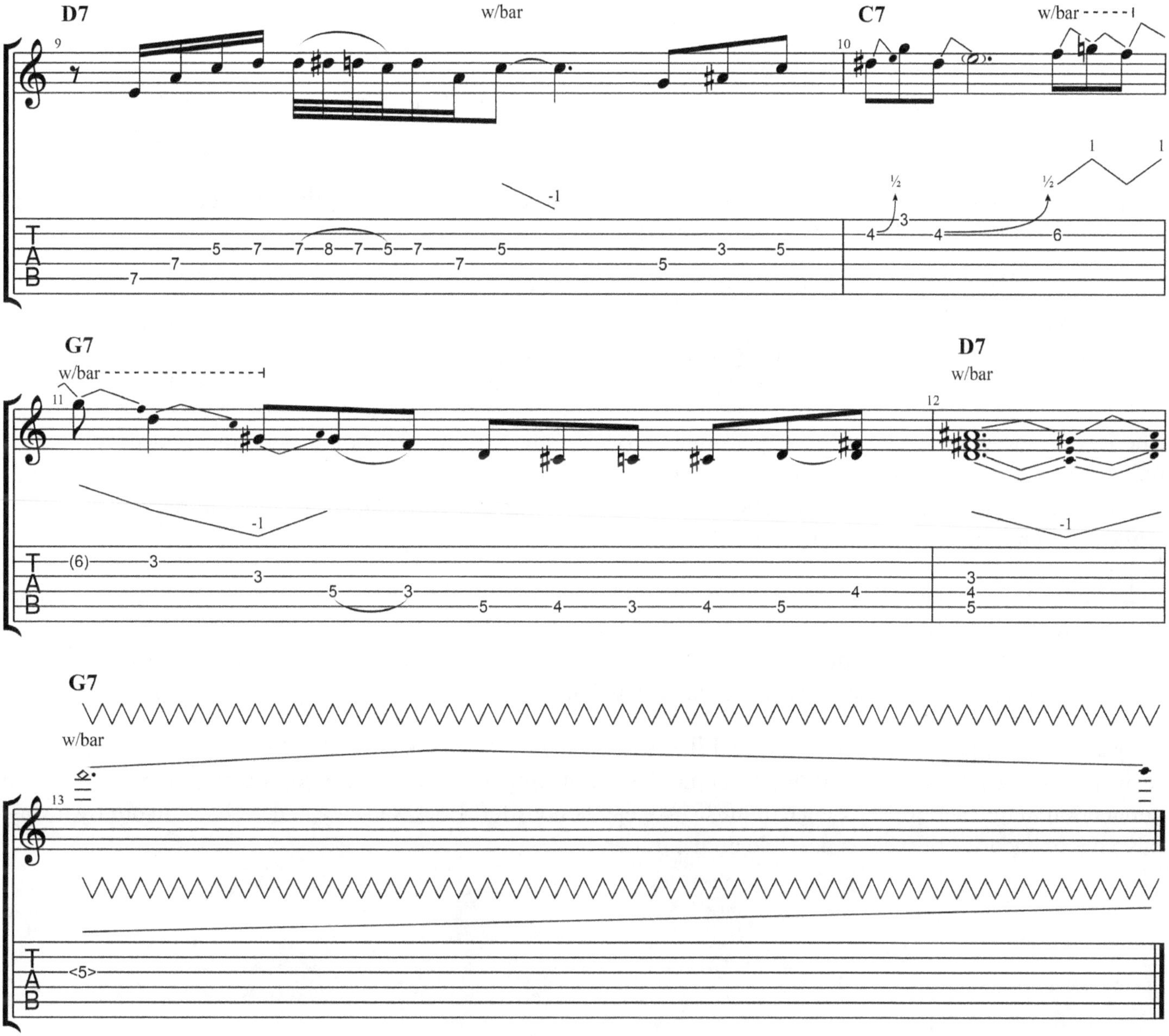
D7
w/bar
C7
w/bar
G7
w/bar
D7
w/bar
G7
w/bar

Conclusion

As we conclude our exploration of the profound impact of Jeff Beck's playing, it's clear that his legacy transcends mere guitar techniques. Beck's contribution to the world of music is testament to his innovation, emotional expression, and technical mastery. Beck was a musical alchemist who was able to transform simple notes into profound musical statements. His fearless experimentation with sound and texture, tone and dynamics, and an unparalleled ability to make the guitar *sing,* have left an indelible mark.

Through the detailed examination of his playing methods, including his unique use of the whammy bar, application of polyrhythms, sublime phrasing, control of harmonics, and other advanced articulation techniques, we've uncovered a treasure trove of insights that guitarists can work on integrating into their playing for years to come. It's a roadmap for any guitarist who desires to develop their own expressive capabilities.

The key lesson readers can take away from Jeff Beck's musical journey is the importance of developing a unique voice on the instrument. Jeff's willingness to explore diverse musical genres, from rock and blues to jazz to Eastern influences and beyond, meant that he continually broadened his musical horizons – all the while reminding us that technical skills should always serve the music.

Indeed, the most important lesson of Jeff Beck's legacy is to have the courage to be yourself musically. Beck was never just a mere technician, he was first and foremost a storyteller; someone who used the guitar to convey emotions that words could not. He challenged conventions, experimented relentlessly with sound, and ultimately expanded the vocabulary of the electric guitar.

As we reflect on Beck's contributions and the lessons shared here, it's clear that his influence will continue to inspire musicians for generations to come. Through diligent practice, creative exploration, and a deep connection to the emotional essence of music, we can honour Jeff Beck's legacy and perhaps, in our own way, push the boundaries of what is possible on the guitar.

www.ingramcontent.com/pod-product-compliance
Lightning Source LLC
Chambersburg PA
CBHW081433090426
42740CB00017B/3286